SPACE ROCKET

Editorial: Steve Parker
Design: David West
Children's Book Design
Illustrator: Simon Bishop & Ron Hayward
Picture research: Cecilia Weston-Baker
Consultant: Brian Jones (Astronomy & space flight, writer and broadcaster)

Created and designed by
N. W. Books Ltd
70 Old Compton Street
London W1

First published in the
United States in 1988 by
Gloucester Press
387 Park Avenue South
New York, NY 10016

ISBN 0-531-17099-3

Library of Congress Catalog
Card Number: 88-50517

Printed in Belgium

Contents

ENGINEERS AT WORK

SPACE ROCKET

TIM FURNISS

GLOUCESTER PRESS

New York · London · Toronto · Sydney

THE ROCKET

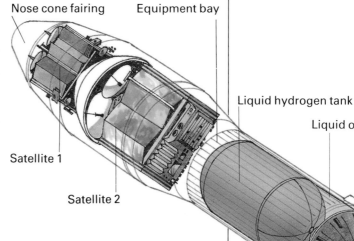

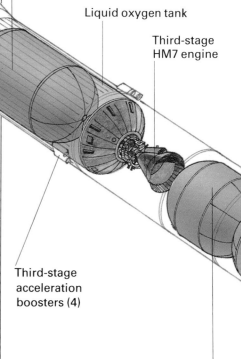

Nose cone fairing   Equipment bay

Satellite 1

Satellite 2

Liquid hydrogen tank

Liquid oxygen tank

Third-stage
HM7 engine

Third-stage
acceleration
boosters (4)

Nitrogen tetroxide tank

Frenchman Jules Verne wrote books about space travel, such as *From the Earth to the Moon* (1870) shown here. A century later, the real thing happened. But the U.S. Apollo mooncraft looked very different from the rocket imagined by Verne!

In our modern world, engineering and technology are becoming more and more complex. Researchers develop new metals, plastics and other materials with amazing properties. Electronics experts make advances in computers almost weekly. At the center of design and construction are the engineers. Their work today will solve the problems posed by tomorrow's great buildings and giant machines, from skyscrapers to bridges, power stations, cars, airliners – and space rockets.

Some 30 years ago, the Space Age was just beginning. It was an era of firsts: first satellite in 1957, first astronaut in 1961, and first steps on the Moon in 1969. There are still firsts: when will man reach another planet? But there are new types of problems for engineers to solve – because space is now big business. Rockets are regular launch vehicles for satellites and other craft owned by companies in radio, television, weather forecasting, land surveys . . . and, of course, the military. Space is the last frontier, the ultimate engineering challenge.

Ariane
Europe's Ariane rocket is a marvel of complex engineering. During the early years of the Space Age, most satellites and other spacecraft were launched on U.S. or Soviet rockets. But quickly the uses of space grew, such as communications and weather satellites. So engineers from other countries developed rockets, too. In 1973, 10 European countries joined to develop Ariane. It can launch several satellites, packed into its bulging nose.

Many types of rocket have been developed. The first to launch satellites were based on military intercontinental ballistic missiles (ICBMs, above left). Newer versions send probes such as Giotto (center) into deep space. US engineers have designed a partly re-usable rocket, the Space Shuttle (right).

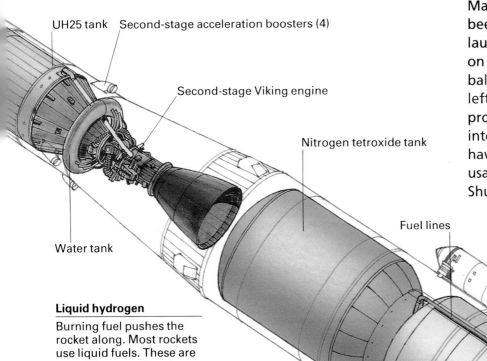

UH25 tank

Second-stage acceleration boosters (4)

Second-stage Viking engine

Nitrogen tetroxide tank

Water tank

Fuel lines

First-stage Viking engines (4)

Water tank

Liquid hydrogen

Burning fuel pushes the rocket along. Most rockets use liquid fuels. These are normally gases, but they are made so cold that they turn to liquid. Liquid hydrogen's temperature is minus 235°C (minus 390°F)!

Liquid oxygen

For the fuel to burn, it needs oxygen. There is no air in space, and so no oxygen. The rocket must take its own supply – the oxidizer. This is usually in liquid form to save space.

UH25 tank

Strap-on boosters (2)

Stabilizing fins

Heatshield

PROBLEMS OF SPACE

Space is a harsh, alien environment that provides many engineering challenges. Spacecraft need to withstand conditions here on Earth, as they are built, and then the rigors away from our planet. In space, temperature in sunlight is 464°F, but in shadow it is minus 400°F! Materials must stand up to such a difference without expanding or contracting too much.

Space is a vacuum, with no air. So a torn spacesuit or leaky craft means death for an astronaut. And on Earth, our atmosphere protects us from deadly cosmic radiation. Yet in space these rays "shine" at full power, damaging any unprotected living thing. Another hazard is the rocky meteors that fly at random through the vacuum. As they approach Earth they burn up in the atmosphere as shooting stars. But in space they are like bullets, making holes in unprotected equipment.

There is no gravity in space. This means an astronaut floats as though weightless. It may seem fun at first. But it can cause problems, as when the astronaut is trying to operate delicate equipment.

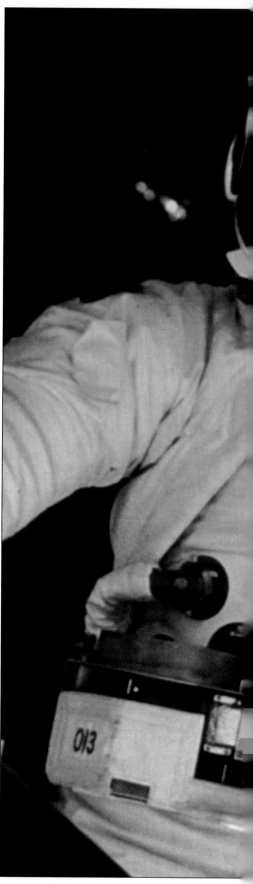

The temperature changes of space, hundreds of degrees in a few minutes, can play havoc with equipment. In the Skylab mission (1973) a panel tore off shortly after launch. The astronauts had to rig up a reflective shield, to protect themselves and the delicate machinery.

Weightlessness can be awkward. Anything not fixed down floats about. Astronauts practice in weightlessness simulated by an aircraft flying up and over in an arc (inset). This gives some idea of what a real spacewalk will feel like.

HOW HIGH IS SPACE?

Officially, space begins 100km (60 miles) above our planet. The Earth's layer of air, the atmosphere, is densest near the ground and fades with height. Temperature also changes with height (shown below).

1 Troposphere (minus 58°F)
2 Stratosphere (32°F)
3 Mesosphere (minus 103°F)
4 Thermosphere (435 to 2,700°F)

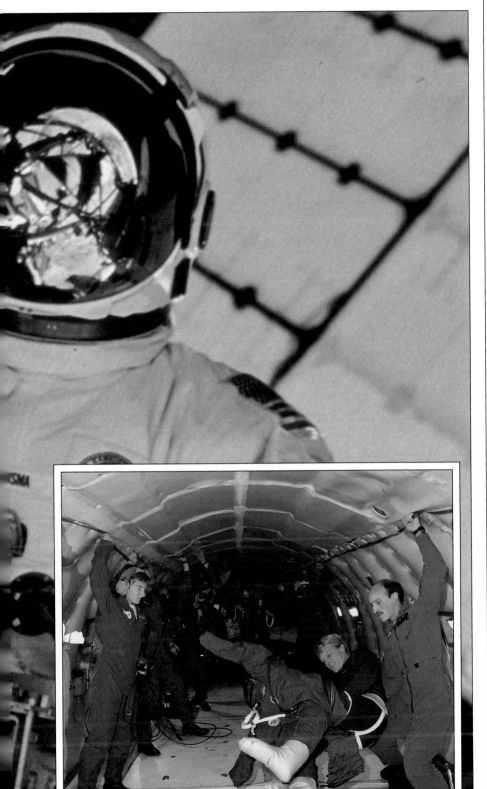

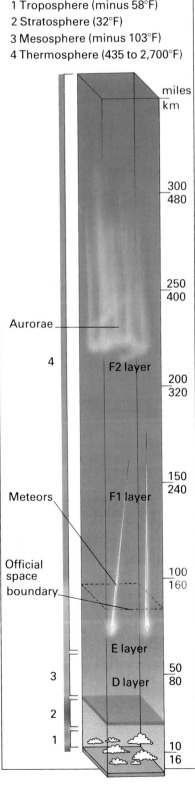

miles
km

300
480

250
400

Aurorae

4   F2 layer
200
320

150
240

Meteors   F1 layer

Official
space
boundary
100
160

E layer
50
80

3   D layer

2

1
10
16

ROCKET ENGINE

A rocket is not propelled forwards by the explosive gases rushing from its engine pushing against the surrounding air. For a start, there is no air in space. Three centuries ago the great English scientist Isaac Newton explained it this way: "For every action, there is an equal and opposite reaction." If a shot-putter wearing ice skates throws the shot forward, he moves backward because of the momentum he has created, not because of the shot pushing against the air. Action-and-reaction is the principle of the rocket engine.

A working rocket engine is a "controlled explosion." It burns fuel in an oxidizer (usually oxygen), in a combustion chamber. This creates hot gases under enormous pressure. The gases accelerate out of the back of the chamber. Engineers found that by making a small exit, or throat, from the chamber, the gases accelerate even more, giving extra thrust. They then added a conical nozzle to the throat. This restricts the gases and accelerates them still more, and also helps with guiding the rocket.

Liquid hydrogen tank

The propellant (fuel and oxidizer) tanks are made of specially developed aluminum alloys. They are shaped like giant aerosol cans since they are designed to do the same job – withstand high pressure from within. As the propellants are consumed and the tanks gradually empty, sloshing about of their contents has to be overcome.

THE ENGINE SYSTEMS

The principle of a rocket engine is simple, but there are many practical problems. Engineers have designed various systems to overcome these. In the Space Shuttle main engine, oxygen oxidizer and hydrogen fuel are first pressurized, mixed and preburned, to form hot gases. These gases are then introduced together in an exact mixture in the combustion chamber. The ultracold fuel circulates in a heat-exchanger, to warm itself before preburning and to cool the chamber and nozzle.

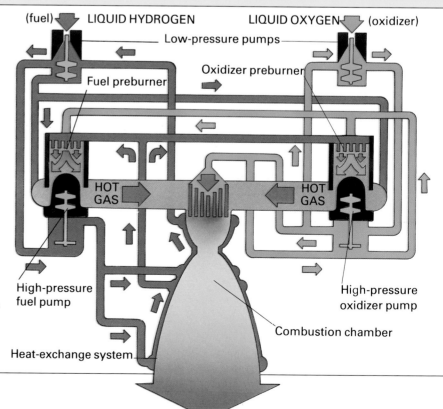

(fuel) LIQUID HYDROGEN   LIQUID OXYGEN (oxidizer)
Low-pressure pumps
Fuel preburner
Oxidizer preburner
HOT GAS   HOT GAS
High-pressure fuel pump
High-pressure oxidizer pump
Combustion chamber
Heat-exchange system

STAYING UPRIGHT

A fully-loaded rocket is not very stable. A guidance system must balance it and keep it on course, like someone balancing a long pole on the palm of the hand. Otherwise the rocket might suffer structural failure, break up and explode, or even topple over and head back to Earth! The latest development is the laser gyroscope, which remains steady and detects any movements away from the programmed course. The rocket is then steered by gimbals, special joints mounted on the engine or its nozzle. These swivel to direct the propelling gases in the right direction.

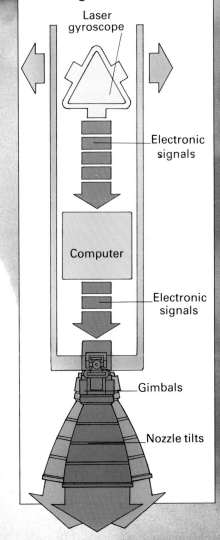

Laser gyroscope

Electronic signals

Computer

Electronic signals

Gimbals

Nozzle tilts

3, 2, 1 . . . IGNITION . . . TAKE OFF

From ignition of Ariane's first-stage engines to takeoff (T0) is 3.4 seconds. There follows a precise program of events in which every split second counts . . . and every split second is counted. T+42 secs: solid rocket boosters burn out and fall away. T+143 secs: liquid boosters fall away. T+203 secs (3.4 mins): first stage shuts down. T+333 secs: second stage shuts down. T+1,058 secs (17.6 mins): third stage puts satellite into preliminary orbit. Then each satellite's engines fire to finalize its orbit.

PAYLOADS

A *payload* is a rocket's item of cargo – whatever it takes into space, from a small satellite to a large space station. Since the Space Age began in 1957, more than 3,500 payloads have been launched. Some were sent into various orbits around the Earth, others went to the Moon and the planets. Some of these payloads were launched together on the same rocket.

In 1958, a U.S. Juno 1 rocket launched an Explorer satellite weighing just 30 pounds. In 1987, the Soviet Energia rocket carried a 100-ton payload. The average telecommunications satellite weighs about 2.5 tons. In the early days, rockets were developed to carry one type of payload, and subsequent cargoes were designed to fit the rocket. Today, rockets such as Ariane come in "families," with a range of abilities depending on what the customer needs. In the early 1980s, Ariane 1 lifted payloads of 1.75 tons into preliminary orbit. Ariane 5 should lift almost 10 tons. The rocket has become a launch vehicle or "launcher," just one link in modern space technology.

Space stations

The Soviet Proton rocket was introduced in 1965 for "heavy lifts." Early versions carried the Salyut space stations. More recently it has been used to raise the 21-ton Mir space station into low Earth orbit. Proton can also take payloads weighing more than 2 tons to the higher geostationary orbit, and can take heavier payloads to the Moon, Venus and Mars.

There are about 20 different types of launch vehicle in use today around the globe. Some carry military payloads, some launch manned spacecraft, and some are commercial vehicles which compete for the launching business.

Military satellites

The U.S. Titan "family" can launch up to eight small military satellites or two larger ones. These are carried into low Earth orbit, only a few hundred miles above the surface. If the satellites need to go into geostationary orbit (page 14), a two-part upper stage fires to boost them thousands more miles into space.

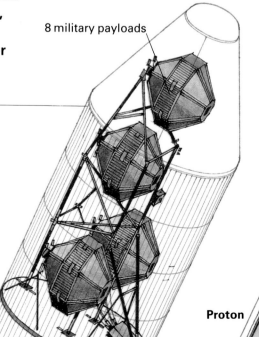

8 military payloads

Mir space station

Titan IIIC

Proton

The Marecs A satellite, launched by an Ariane 1 in 1981, is carefully prepared in dust-free surroundings.

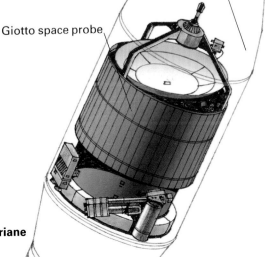

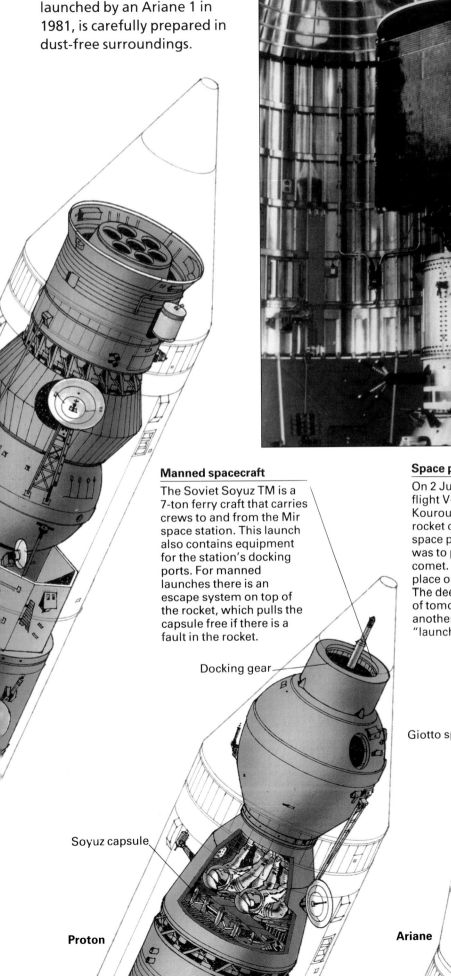

Manned spacecraft

The Soviet Soyuz TM is a 7-ton ferry craft that carries crews to and from the Mir space station. This launch also contains equipment for the station's docking ports. For manned launches there is an escape system on top of the rocket, which pulls the capsule free if there is a fault in the rocket.

Docking gear

Soyuz capsule

Proton

Space probes

On 2 July 1985, Ariane flight V-14 blasted off from Kourou. The Ariane type 1 rocket carried the Giotto space probe. Its mission was to pass near Halley's comet. The flypast took place on 13 March 1986. The deep-space meetings of tomorrow are yet another task for today's "launchers".

Giotto space probe

Ariane

IN ORBIT

In orbit around the Earth, a satellite's forward speed gives it an outward force which equals and counteracts the Earth's gravity pulling it back. It is always "falling" towards the Earth, yet moving forwards fast enough to keep going. Getting into orbit is the rocket's main job. The next problem is: Which orbit? There are an infinite number, from a few hundred to many thousands of miles high, from circular to elliptical, from over the Equator to over the Poles.

Communications satellites need a perfectly circular orbit 36,000 kilometers (22,400 miles) above the Earth. At this height their speed is 1,685 km/h (1050 mph) – which matches the rotation of the Earth beneath. So they appear to "hang" over one spot on the Earth's surface. This is a geostationary orbit, and transmitters and receivers can be locked onto the satellite. However, an Earth observation satellite may work best in a lower, faster orbit over the Poles. By placing the satellite in such an orbit, engineers ensure that it "sees" the whole globe in 24 hours, as the Earth rotates beneath.

Reaching GTO

Ariane's third stage takes its "comsats into GTO" -- that is, its communication satellites are taken into geostationary transfer orbit about the Earth.

In stable spin

Once in GTO, the engineers have 400 seconds to launch the satellites. First they spin the stage and its satellites, to make the flight more stable.

Separation 1

At the critical moment, the first satellite separates. Then the third stage slows its spin and changes its orientation, to prepare for the separation of the second satellite.

Casing ejected

The casing of the second satellite is ejected and another spin stabilization begins. The second satellite and the tilt of the third stage are checked before separation.

A Meteosat weather satellite in geostationary orbit is high above the Earth, which is 12,750 km (7,920 mi) across.

The geostationary transfer orbit (inset) is elliptical, only 240 km (150 mi) high at its lowest point.

STAYING IN ORBIT

European Telecom-munications Satellite Organization's Eutelsat is one of dozens of satellites in geostationary orbit. It should remain above one position on Earth, its aerials pointing exactly at ground stations. It must stay in its own geostationary orbit, to prevent colliding with other satellites. But even in the stillness of space, craft move. Solar wind and other radiation can push them out of position. Small thrusters on the satellite keep it in exact position, under command from the ground, if the satellite's signals begin to fade or wander.

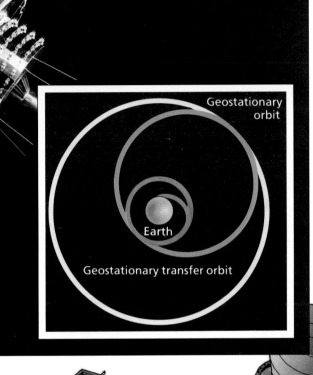

Geostationary orbit

Earth

Geostationary transfer orbit

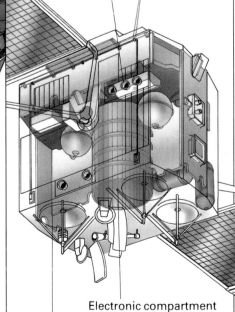

Solar energy panels

Positioning thrusters

Electronic compartment

Dish radio aerials

Separation 2

The second satellite is released from the third stage and goes on its way. Small boosters on each satellite then push them from GTO into full geostationary orbit.

Collision avoidance

Its main job is now done, but the third stage rocket has one last task. It boosts once more, flying out of orbit and into space, so that it will not collide with a satellite.

MAN IN SPACE

Over 200 people have traveled into space. The first astronauts made solo flights lasting a few hours, but today's flights by certain Soviet crew members may last up to a year. Living in space presents the engineer with many problems. The space station needs to be specially equipped and supplied regularly. It needs fresh food, drinkable water, clean air and electrical power. There must be enough experiments and activities to keep the crew busy. They also need comfortable rest areas where they can enjoy privacy and entertain themselves with videos and music.

Experience has shown that exercise for crew members is a vital need. In the weightlessness of space, and in the confines of a small craft, normal work activity is not enough. Two hours of vigorous exercise are needed each day. Otherwise an astronaut's bones become brittle, and his muscles might weaken so much that he could die when he returned to Earth's gravity. Engineers have to take all these factors into consideration when they design space vehicles that people will live in.

For the first few days in space, many astronauts feel dizzy or sick. This is because the balancing mechanism inside the ear is affected by weightlessness, rather like being seasick. And without gravity to tense the muscles, body posture becomes hunched. Exercising with constraints to simulate gravity helps to keep muscles from wasting.

Mir, the Soviet space station, is a self-contained home in space, orbiting the Earth. One crew member lived here for over 320 days.

Power from the Sun

Fold-out panels on the space station contain silicon solar cells. These collect the Sun's rays and convert their energy into electricity that powers the equipment.

Recycled air

Air in the station can be recycled for a time. It is freshened by circulating through filters which remove the carbon dioxide.

Shirtsleeve conditions

Crew members live and work in a "shirtsleeve" environment. They only wear spacesuits if they go outside. The station is protected by a meteorite shield.

Regular supplies

A Progress unmanned tanker docks with Mir and delivers fresh fuel, water and air tanks. It may also carry food, scientific equipment and the latest video and music tapes.

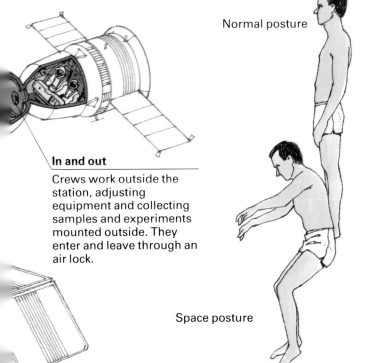

Exercising in zero gravity

Normal posture

Space posture

In and out

Crews work outside the station, adjusting equipment and collecting samples and experiments mounted outside. They enter and leave through an air lock.

LIVING IN "ZERO G"

Weightlessness is sometimes called "zero g," meaning the force of gravity (g) is zero. It presents many problems, since things float about if not fixed in some way – from a screwdriver to water used for washing. Engineers on the U.S. Space Shuttle have come up with some ingenious solutions, shown below. The gadgets are a vacuum-shower (top) and a toilet (center). Even mealtimes (bottom) must be crumb-free!

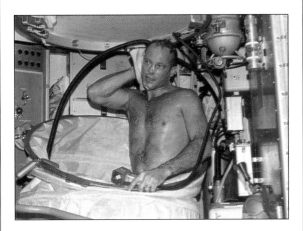

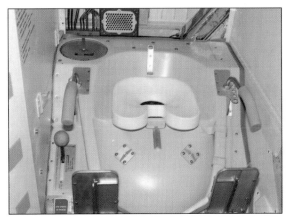

WORKING IN SPACE

Ability to work outside the spacecraft is vital to today's space missions. Repairs may need to be made on the outside. Experiments in the space environment need to be carried out and samples retrieved. Sometimes a rogue satellite must be captured and repaired. Occasionally, a space rescue is necessary.

To work outside the craft, the astronaut needs his own "personal spacecraft" – the spacesuit. This is a miracle of design and engineering. It protects the wearer from the airless conditions filled with radiation and tiny meteors. It

The human satellite.
A U.S. astronaut orbits the Earth (right), free from attaching ropes. He is, in effect, an independent satellite with his own particular orbit. But before the astronaut goes out into space he must spend hours preparing and putting on the various parts of the spacesuit, as shown below.

Undergarments

To stay cool in the suit, the astronaut wears water-cooled underwear. He breathes pure oxygen to prevent the "bends," which deep-sea divers also get.

The urge to go

The astronaut does not want to waste valuable time coming in to use the toilet. So a urine receptacle is provided in the suit. He also wears a solid waste receptacle.

Overgarments

The outer part of the spacesuit comes in sections, so that it is easier to put on. Each joint must be gastight, to prevent the pressurized air inside from leaking away.

Backpack

A portable life-support system is contained in a "backpack." It provides oxygen, cleans the breathed-out air by filters, and circulates cooling water.

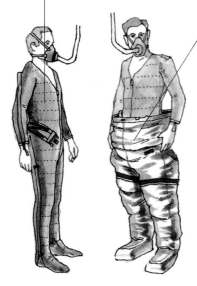

shields him from great temperature changes as he moves from sunshine to shadow. It provides recirculated air to breathe. A small rocket pack enables him to move around without an attaching line. Engineers must make sure the suit allows easy, unrestricted movements. Special joints let the legs and elbows bend. The suit must be easy to put on, too. A badly designed spacesuit could exhaust an astronaut even before he gets outside!

Two-way talking

The astronaut needs to communicate while outside, so he uses a helmet with a microphone attached. The spacesuit helmet itself may contain a small drink with a straw, and a bite-sized candy bar, for in-space refreshment.

Handy equipment

Gloves are a special challenge. They must protect, stay pressurized, yet be flexible enough to work comfortably.

Helmet

The plastic laminate helmet is extremely tough. The tinted visor allows good visibility but protects the eyes against intense sunlight.

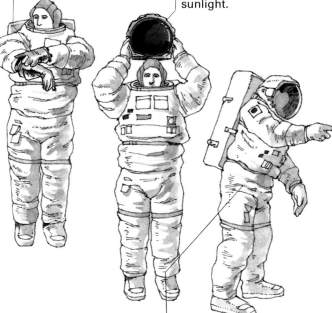

Ready to leave

The astronaut is ready to leave the craft for EVA (extravehicular activity). He enters an air lock and opens the door to space.

THE HUMAN ROCKET

The astronaut in space moves around using a MMU (manned maneuvering unit) on the backpack. This allows him to travel backward, forward, sideways, up and down, and to tilt and roll around. He moves two hand control units, and his motions are translated by a computer which operates small gas thrusters. The astronaut may also have a special attachment unit allowing him to join up with a rogue satellite. He can then bring the satellite to the spacecraft for repair.

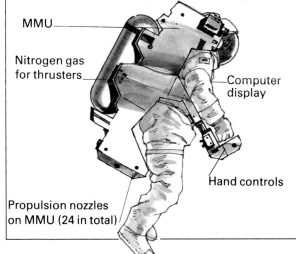

MMU

Nitrogen gas for thrusters

Computer display

Hand controls

Propulsion nozzles on MMU (24 in total)

SPACE PROBES

Space probes explore well away from our world. They travel to the planets and moons and voyage deep into space. The first engineering requirement is a rocket that will launch the probe to *escape velocity*, so that it can break free from the grasp of the Earth's gravity. The probe is then put into an orbit around the Sun. This is carefully calculated so that many months or years later, it will meet up with its target planet. Such accuracy must be

The U.S. Voyager 2 was launched in 1977. It has already visited Jupiter, Saturn and Uranus, and will tour Neptune in 1989 – before leaving the solar system for ever.

Signals across space

When Voyager sent back its radio signals from Uranus, they took 2 hours 45 minutes to reach Earth. The large dish aerial is used to detect and focus weak signals sent out from Earth, which of course take just as long to reach Voyager. These signals instruct the probe to change its position, for example, or switch on a camera.

Deep-space camera

The probe's "cameras" do not actually take photographs. Rather they are imaging systems that perform line-by-line scans of the subject. The scans are converted into electrical signals. These are transmitted to Earth and are built up into a picture. Besides detecting light, cameras may also "see" other wavelengths such as X-rays.

In-flight maneuvers

Thrusters are vital for small changes in course and position, and especially during the computer-controlled flypast of a planet. Not only must the probe's cameras be pointing toward the planet, but the aerial needs to be pointing back to Earth! The 16 thrusters use hydrazine propellant.

Thruster fuel tank

Uranus Jan 24, 1986

Power in the darkness

As a probe travels to the edge of the solar system, the Sun becomes just another star (although a very bright one). So solar panels cannot be used to create electricity from the Sun's energy. Engineers have devised nuclear powerpacks, which convert the energy of radioactive plutonium into electricity. These work for many years.

programmed into the probe. Fine tuning of the course can be achieved by firing small thrusters on the probe's outside.

Each world visited presents its own problems to the engineer. Mercury is intensely hot. There is tremendous pressure on the surface of Venus. Mars has raging dust storms. Jupiter is bathed in strong radiation. Saturn is surrounded by its rings and other whirling space debris. And there is the sheer cold of Uranus. Yet within 30 years of the start of the Space Age, probes had successfully visited all these planets in our solar system. It is a testimony to the skills of the engineers.

It would take perhaps 100 years for a spacecraft to reach Uranus under its own power. But with careful flight planning, it can use the "slingshot effect." In this, the gravitational force of a planet almost catches the probe and then flings it on its way. By using the gravity of Jupiter and Saturn, Voyager vastly increased its speed. The ingenious "slingshot" has helped us to explore the solar system so quickly.

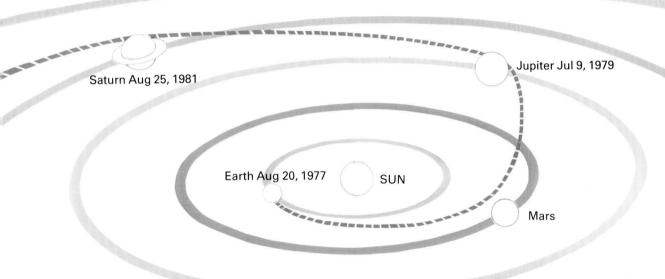

Saturn Aug 25, 1981

Jupiter Jul 9, 1979

Earth Aug 20, 1977

SUN

Mars

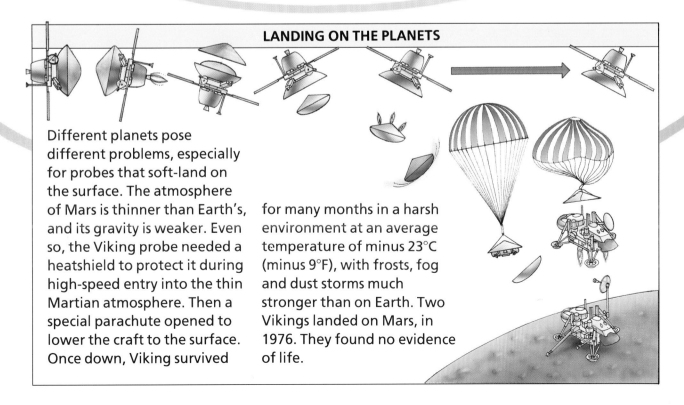

LANDING ON THE PLANETS

Different planets pose different problems, especially for probes that soft-land on the surface. The atmosphere of Mars is thinner than Earth's, and its gravity is weaker. Even so, the Viking probe needed a heatshield to protect it during high-speed entry into the thin Martian atmosphere. Then a special parachute opened to lower the craft to the surface. Once down, Viking survived for many months in a harsh environment at an average temperature of minus 23°C (minus 9°F), with frosts, fog and dust storms much stronger than on Earth. Two Vikings landed on Mars, in 1976. They found no evidence of life.

REENTRY

Satellites do not orbit the Earth forever. The planet's gravity eventually pulls back most satellites in low orbit. As they reenter the Earth's atmosphere, their work done, they burn up like shooting stars. But manned spacecraft need to return to Earth safely in one piece, at a certain time and place.

Reentry is a great problem for the engineers. The spacecraft is traveling so fast, about 27,000 km/h (17,000 mph), that as it reaches the upper layers of the Earth's atmosphere there is enormous friction with the thin air. The friction generates intense heat. Heatshields have been developed that *ablate*, or burn away, to absorb and deflect the heat. Other types of shield do not burn away but reflect as much heat as possible.

The angle of entry into the atmosphere is crucial. If the spacecraft enters at an angle that is too steep then, even with a heatshield, the craft could become too hot and burn up. If the angle is too shallow, the craft could "bounce off" the outer atmosphere and fly away out of control, into space.

1 Retrofire

Gagarin's spacecraft, Vostok, made a single orbit of Earth. The Vostok program was headed by Soviet chief space engineer Sergei Korolev. To prepare for reentry, Vostok's retro-rocket (one pointing forward) fires to reduce its speed. The Earth's gravity begins to pull down the craft.

All U.S. manned spacecraft that flew before the Space Shuttle splashed down in the sea. Sometimes the capsule turned upside down and had to be righted using buoyancy bags. Here, Apollo astronauts have joined rescue divers in their boat. Heat scars on the capsule show the rigors of reentry.

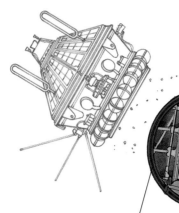

2 Alignment

Gagarin sits in his capsule, a sphere about 2.3 meters (7.5 feet) across. The instrument section of the craft aligns the capsule perfectly so that it will reenter the atmosphere at the correct angle and not burn up, and then fly the right path to the landing zone. The instrument section then separates from the capsule. Gagarin himself is more a passenger than a pilot and has little to do – operations are automatic or controlled from Earth.

4 Pilot ejects

The 2.4-ton Vostok capsule plummets to the ground at high speed, the main heat of reentry over. But even with a parachute, its landing will be too fast and hard for a person. Gagarin must eject and land separately. He bails out at a height of 6,000 meters (3.7 miles) and floats to Earth on his own parachute.

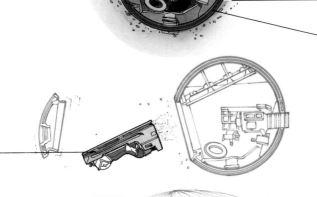

3 Reentry

Traveling at about 20 times the speed of sound, the capsule flies into the atmosphere and glows like a blowtorch. The heatshield absorbs much of the heat and burns away, protecting the human passenger inside. Gagarin is on course to land near the River Volga.

5 Landing

At first, Soviet authorities said that Gagarin had stayed in his capsule until it landed on the ground. But later this was shown to be untrue. All the Vostok astronauts ejected at about 6,000 meters (3.7 miles). However in later Soviet space programs the astronauts did indeed land on the ground, still inside their capsules. This was made possible because the capsules were equipped with retro-rockets to cushion the landing impact.

In 1961, Soviet pilot Yuri Gagarin became the first human in space. His flight lasted 1 hour 48 minutes. This is how he returned.

THE REUSABLE ROCKET

An airliner is not thrown away or put in a museum after just one flight. Yet this happened to spacecraft for 20 years of manned spaceflight – until the arrival of the U.S. Space Shuttle. At first, Shuttle engineers were given the job of designing a totally reusable launcher-and-spaceplane system. But engineering constraints are not only technological, they can also be financial. Cuts in the budget made it impossible to design a fully reusable system. The engineers eventually came up with today's Shuttle.

The Shuttle has four main parts. The spaceplane itself, or *orbiter*, has three main engines. At takeoff it has two solid-fuel boosters that burn out and separate 2 minutes 12 seconds later. The boosters fall back to Earth with parachutes, and many of their parts can be reused. There is also a giant external tank which supplies propellants to the orbiter's three engines. This separates 8 minutes 50 seconds after takeoff. The tank is not reusable, burning up on reentry. Its mission over, the orbiter glides down.

The Shuttle orbiter lands on a runway, like an airliner. Five orbiters were built. Enterprise was only used for tests in the atmosphere. Columbia was first into space, on April 12, 1981. On January 28, 1986, Challenger blew up less than two minutes after takeoff. The seven crew were killed. The Shuttle program was grounded while engineers looked for the fault.

One key to the Shuttle's re-usability is its covering of tiles and blankets. These are made of special ceramic materials (far right), designed to withstand temperatures up to 2,500°F without damage.

SHUTTLE TO SPACE AND BACK

On the launch pad, the entire Space Shuttle weighs about 2,000 tons. The orbiter itself is 122 feet long and 78 feet from one wingtip to the other. As it lands, it is the world's biggest glider. The giant propellant tank that forms the orbiter's nose is 154 feet high and 27.5 feet across. It carries 709 tons of liquids, both propellant and oxidizer, for the orbiter's main engines. The boosters are 149 feet tall and 12.1 feet across.

External tank contains propellants for orbiter's main engines

Flight deck for pilot and co-pilot

Living quarters for up to 10 people

Cargo bay can carry almost 30 tons of payloads per mission

2 small engines for maneuvering in space

Orbiter's 3 main engines

Solid-fuel boosters

Orbiter's fuel

Liquid oxygen

Liquid hydrogen

Solid fuel

NASA

United States

THE FUTURE . . ?

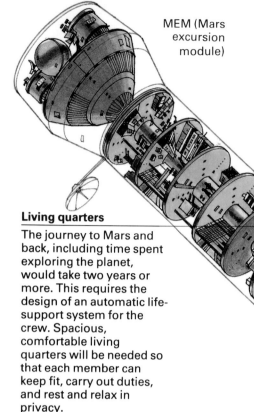

MEM (Mars excursion module)

Today, designers and engineers are already planning the next advances in space technology and travel. Early next century, they should have developed new breeds of spacecraft. Earth orbit transporters, the new Space Shuttles, will be fully reusable. There may be a manned spaceship on its way to Mars, using a new method of propulsion. Automatic space tugs may be ferrying supplies and equipment between Earth and permanently manned space stations. By the year 2020, there could be manned bases on the Moon.

Each new development will be the result of the engineers' work. They are continually researching into new materials, fuels and technologies, to make the dreams of today come true tomorrow. They do not work in isolation. Many developments in space have come from new technologies in more Earthbound areas such as nuclear power stations. Also, space research has created benefits for Earthlings – from the making of medicines in ultrapure, gravity-free surroundings to the coating on a nonstick frying pan!

Living quarters

The journey to Mars and back, including time spent exploring the planet, would take two years or more. This requires the design of an automatic life-support system for the crew. Spacious, comfortable living quarters will be needed so that each member can keep fit, carry out duties, and rest and relax in privacy.

Hotol is Britain's planned re-usable spaceplane. It will use oxygen from the atmosphere, during the first part of its flight. It could become the first spacecraft to reach Earth orbit as a single-stage vehicle.

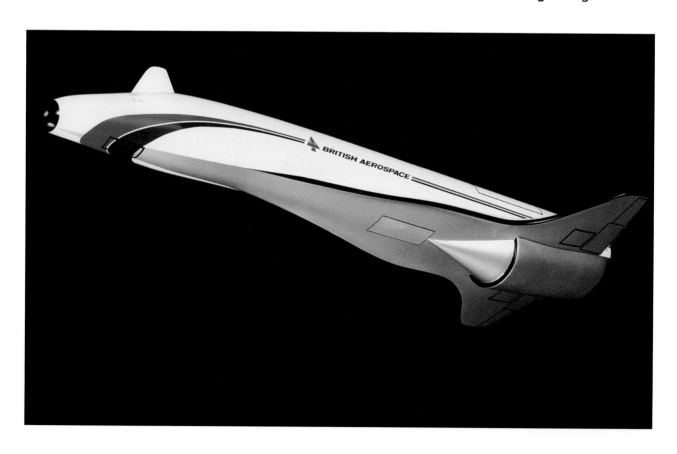

On a Mars trip, high-performance engines send the expedition craft from Earth orbit (1) into an elliptical orbit around the Sun (2). The spacecraft enters Mars orbit (3) and a lander descends to the surface. Later it takes off and rejoins the mother ship (4). On the way back, the gravity of the planet Venus (5) slows the craft before it reaches Earth (6).

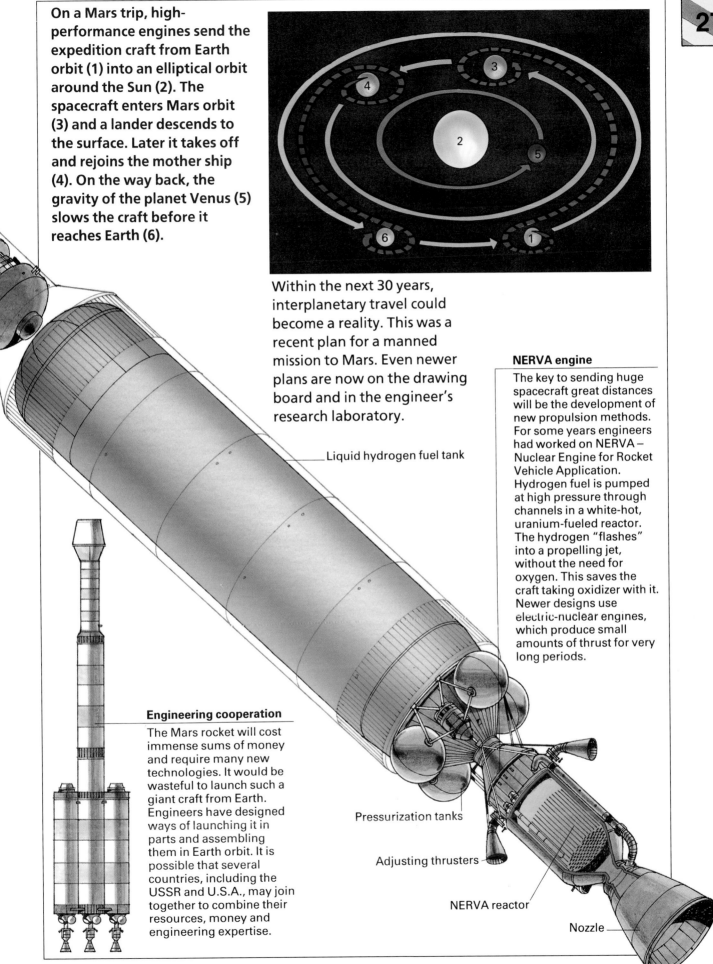

Within the next 30 years, interplanetary travel could become a reality. This was a recent plan for a manned mission to Mars. Even newer plans are now on the drawing board and in the engineer's research laboratory.

Liquid hydrogen fuel tank

NERVA engine

The key to sending huge spacecraft great distances will be the development of new propulsion methods. For some years engineers had worked on NERVA – Nuclear Engine for Rocket Vehicle Application. Hydrogen fuel is pumped at high pressure through channels in a white-hot, uranium-fueled reactor. The hydrogen "flashes" into a propelling jet, without the need for oxygen. This saves the craft taking oxidizer with it. Newer designs use electric-nuclear engines, which produce small amounts of thrust for very long periods.

Engineering cooperation

The Mars rocket will cost immense sums of money and require many new technologies. It would be wasteful to launch such a giant craft from Earth. Engineers have designed ways of launching it in parts and assembling them in Earth orbit. It is possible that several countries, including the USSR and U.S.A., may join together to combine their resources, money and engineering expertise.

Pressurization tanks

Adjusting thrusters

NERVA reactor

Nozzle

THE YOUNG ENGINEER

Spacecraft are in the forefront of technology and are among the most complicated machines ever made. Advances in the 30 years since the Space Age began are staggering. Yet today's space vehicles are based on some of the simplest engineering principles. Try the projects shown here, which show a few of the scientific laws involved in space travel.

Rocket power

Isaac Newton, the great scientist, said that every action has an equal and opposite reaction (page 8). The rocket engine uses this principle. Burning the fuel produces gases that expand with explosive force. These rush out the back of the engine and propel the rocket forwards. Blow up a sausage-shaped balloon and hold the end while you suspend it from a taut length of string using tape. Then let go of the end.

The pressurized air in the balloon rushes backward out of the hole and the balloon should react by shooting forward. Forcing the expanding gases through a limited hole accelerates them to provide extra thrust.

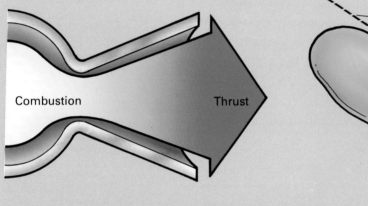

Combustion   Thrust

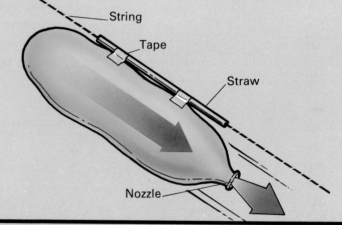

String

Tape

Straw

Nozzle

In orbit

A satellite in orbit has several forces acting on it. There is no air in space, so once the satellite is set in motion, it does not slow down. Obeying the laws of physics, it tends to try and carry on in a straight line. However the Earth's gravity counteracts this by pulling it down. If the satellite's forward speed is correct, it will "fall" endlessly around the Earth (page 14). Show this by twirling a small rubber ball on a string (1). You are gravity, and you can feel the ball's tendency to go in a straight line as the pull in the string. Let go (2), and the ball does just that!

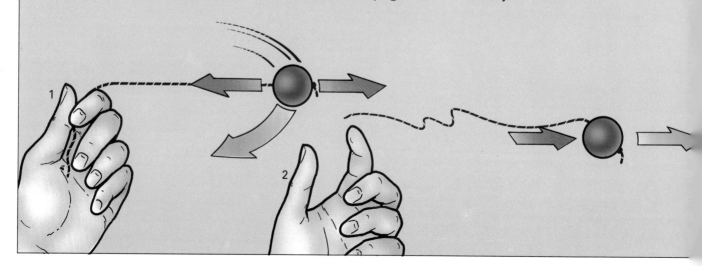

1

2

The heatshield

In the full glare of the Sun, it can be very hot in space. The surface temperature of Mercury reaches 750°F! Spacecraft must be protected against such intense heat (and cold, too). Shiny surfaces reflect heat and protect whatever they cover (page 6). Demonstrate this by making your own "space blanket." Get two large glasses and wrap shiny metal foil around one. Fill them both with water from the cold tap. Check their temperatures with a thermometer and leave them both on a sunny windowsill. Which one stays cool longest? It should be the one wrapped in foil.

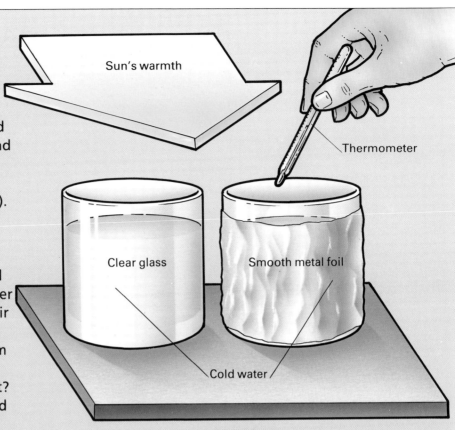

Sun's warmth

Thermometer

Clear glass

Smooth metal foil

Cold water

Reentry angle

One of the most critical parts of any space mission is reentry into Earth's atmosphere. If the craft comes in too steeply, it may "crash" into the outer layers of air at high speed, overheat and burn up (page 22). If the angle is too shallow, the craft may bounce off the upper atmosphere and race off into space. You can demonstrate this by throwing pebbles into water. A pebble hurled low and hard, at a shallow angle, should skip along the surface (1). This is like a spacecraft skipping off the outer atmosphere. Thrown too high, a pebble hits the water almost vertically with a loud splash – like a craft reentering too steeply and burning up. The correct angle is somewhere in between (2). Then the craft's reentry shields can cope with the heat generated, yet it slows down enough to fall through the atmosphere to the ground.

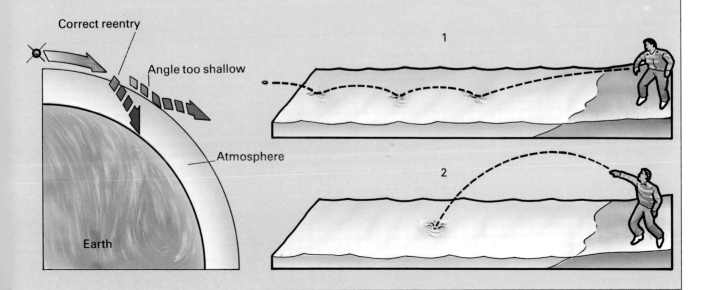

Correct reentry

Angle too shallow

Atmosphere

Earth

1

2

ROCKET DEVELOPMENT

The main era of great "firsts" in space was during the 1960s. In eight years, rocket and payload engineers progressed from putting the first man in space to putting the first man on the Moon.

Today, the days of the "Space Race" are fading. The space programs of various countries proceed at a more measured pace, each with its own long-term goal. The United States has its Space Shuttle program. Europe's Ariane rockets take off regularly, lifting satellites and probes for its member countries and for commercial customers. Japan, China and India have developed launch rockets. The Soviet Union's Energia rocket and Mir space station are major steps forward in conquering interplanetary travel and having permanently-manned bases in space.

In the 1980s, the American "Star Wars" program aimed to put military satellites and vehicles in space. Some feared this would lead to battles in space, while others hoped it would end the threats of nuclear war and destruction of our planet. In 1988, the United States and the Soviet Union discussed the possibility of combining their resources for a manned mission to Mars.

12th century	Chinese use gunpowder rockets to bombard enemies in battle
13th century	Gunpowder and rockets reach Europe and are used in warfare near Venice
18th century	Bamboo rockets fly more than 2 km (1.5 miles) during battles in India
1840s	Englishman William Hales invents spin-stabilized rocket for straighter, more accurate flight
1903	First modern rocket designer, Konstantin Tsiolkovsky (USSR), publishes designs for liquid fuel rockets and says they will work in airless space
1926	Robert Goddard, US rocket designer, launches first liquid-fuel rocket, flies 12.5m (41 ft) high
1931	German Johannes Winkler launches a liquid-fuel rocket to 600m (2,500 ft) high
1933	Soviet rocket designer Friedrich Tsander sends a GIRD X to almost 5 km (3 miles) in altitude
1934	German Werner von Braun sends an A-2 rocket to 2.5 km (1.5 miles) high
1935	A Goddard rocket flies to 2.3 km (1.5 miles)
1944-45	German V-2 rockets bomb Allies in Europe during World War II, with a range of 300 km (200 miles)
1950s	Rockets developed for Intercontinental Ballistic Missiles, with ranges of 8,000 km (5,000 miles) or more
1957	First space satellite, Sputnik 1, launches on Soviet A rocket
1961	Yuri Gagarin (USSR) becomes first man in space on Soviet A-1 rocket
1962	First US orbital space flight made by John Glenn after launch on Atlas rocket
1964	USSR sends first 3-man capsule into space on Soviet A-2 rocket
1965	USSR introduces Proton family of rockets and boosters to launch satellites, manned capsules and Salyut space stations
1967	Saturn V (USA), the world's biggest rocket, becomes operational
1969	Saturn V boosts three US astronauts out of Earth orbit; Neil Armstrong becomes first man on the Moon
1970	China launches its first Long March rocket
1973	European ministers agree to develop their own launch rocket, Ariane
1975	A US Apollo capsule links with a Soviet Soyuz capsule and the astronauts shake hands
1979	Ariane's first test launch is successful
1981	First flight of Space Shuttle (USA), with the orbiter Columbia
1984	Ariane's first commercial launch, carrying Spacenet 1 satellite for GTE organization
1985	In the 14th launch of the program, an Ariane 1 boosts space probe Giotto on its way to meet Halley's comet in 1986
1986	Japan's first launch of its H-1 rocket
1986	Space Shuttle with Challenger orbiter explodes shortly after take-off; 7 crew killed; program postponed for at least 2 years
1987	USSR's Energia, a "heavy lifter," is launched successfully; smaller but more powerful than Saturn V, and capable of putting 100 tons into low Earth orbit, it opens a new era in space station technology and deep-space exploration

GLOSSARY

Ablate To burn away, absorbing heat in the process.

Astronaut A person who travels in space.

Atmosphere The layer of gases around a large body, such as the air around Earth. It is "thickest" near the ground and becomes thinner with height.

Booster A self-contained rocket engine fixed ("strapped on") to a spacecraft to give it extra thrust, for example, on takeoff. It usually separates from the craft when used up.

Cosmonaut A person who travels in space. This word is usually applied to Eastern-bloc people – in the West, space travelers are called *astronauts*.

Escape velocity The speed required to break free from Earth's gravity and head off into space.

Gimbal A swivel joint which allows, for example, a rocket nozzle to move, for guidance purposes.

Gyroscope A device that tends to remain in the same position. It usually has a fast-rotating disk as the stable part.

Helium A gas, much lighter than air, used in airships and in space travel.

Launcher A launch vehicle – a rocket engine (or several engines) that takes a *payload* into space.

Liquid fuel A fuel normally in gas form, but made so cold that it condenses into a liquid, to save space (see also *solid fuel*).

Nitrogen tetroxide N_2O_4 A chemical used as an *oxidizer* in space rocket engines.

Orbit The path taken by a small object going around a larger one, held by its gravity.

Oxidizer A substance that provides the oxygen required when a rocket fuel is burned in the airlessness of space.

Payload An item of cargo, such as a satellite launched by a rocket.

Probe, space An unmanned craft that journeys far from the Earth, to other planets and beyond.

Propellant A substance used to push a rocket or spacecraft along.

Rocket A spacecraft, consisting of *launcher*, *payload* and other parts. Also used for a rocket engine, a device that moves forward when hot gases rush out the back.

Satellite An object that orbits a larger one. The Moon is Earth's natural satellite. In addition there are hundreds of man-made satellites orbiting Earth, such as communications devices and leftover parts of rockets.

Solid fuel A fuel in solid form, often used in *boosters* (see also *liquid fuel*).

Stage One part, or section, of a rocket.

Thruster A small device through which pressurized gas escapes, to reposition a craft or astronaut in space.

UH25 A rocket propellant, 75% Unsymmetrical di-methyl hydrazine and 25% Hydrazine hydrate.

Weightlessness When an object is beyond the gravitational pull of a much larger object (a planet or moon), and so has no gravity acting on it.

INDEX

Photographic Credits:
Cover and pages 5 (right), 6, 7 (inset), 15, 19, 22, 24-25 and 25: NASA; page 4: Mary Evans Library; page 5 (left): Frank Spooner Agency; pages 5 (middle) and 13: European Space Agency; pages 7 and 17 (all): Tim Furniss; page 11: Arianespace; page 23: Royal Observatory Edinburgh/Science Museum; page 26: British Aerospace.